This page is intentionally left blank.

TEN REASONS WHY PASTORS ARE IN DANGER
Copyright © 2020 by Jeff Wolf

All rights reserved. No part of this publication may be reproduced, stored in a retrieval system or transmitted in any form or by any means, electronic, mechanical, photocopying, recording or otherwise without the prior permission of the publisher or in accordance with the provisions of the Copyright, Designs and Patents Act 1988 or under the terms of any licence permitting limited copying issued by the Copyright Licensing Agency.

For information about this title or to order other books and/or electronic media, contact the publisher:

Resurgence Publishing, LLC
PO Box 514
Goshen, OH 45122

All Scripture quotations, unless otherwise indicated, are taken from the Holy Bible, New International Version®, NIV®. Copyright ©1973, 1978, 1984, 2011 by Biblica, Inc.TM Used by permission of Zondervan. All rights reserved worldwide. www.zondervan.com The "NIV" and "New International Version" are trademarks registered in the U.S. Patent and Trademark Office by Biblica, Inc.TM

Scripture quotations marked (ESV) are from the ESV® Bible (The Holy Bible, English Standard Version®), copyright © 2001 by Crossway, a publishing ministry of Good News Publishers. Used by permission. All rights reserved.

Scripture quotations marked (NKJV) are taken from the New King James Version®. Copyright © 1982 by Thomas Nelson. Used by permission. All rights reserved.

Scripture quotations marked (MSG) are taken from THE MESSAGE, copyright © 1993, 2002, 2018 by Eugene H. Peterson. Used by permission of NavPress. All rights reserved. Represented by Tyndale House Publishers, a Division of Tyndale House Ministries.

Library of Congress Control Number: 2020903908

ISBN: 9798617708433

Printed in the United States of America

Jeff Wolf
**TEN REASONS WHY
PASTORS ARE IN DANGER**

*Published by Resurgence Publishing, LLC
Loveland, OH*

Contents

DEDICATION 7

FOREWORD 11

INTRODUCTION 15

BECAUSE THEY HAVE MOMENTS OF WEAKNESS. 20

BECAUSE THEY DEAL WITH CONFLICT. 28

BECAUSE THEY OFTEN FEEL LONELY. 38

BECAUSE SOMETIMES THEY DON'T KNOW WHAT TO DO. 48

BECAUSE THEY HAVE TROUBLE SLEEPING. 58

BECAUSE THEY ARE BLEEDING. 66

BECAUSE THEY GET DISTRACTED. 74

BECAUSE THEY LACK CONFIDENCE. 84

BECAUSE SOMETIMES THEY GET AFRAID. 94

BECAUSE THEY NEGLECT THEMSELVES. 102

CONCLUSION 108

Dedication

This book is dedicated to my Dad, David R. Wolf, who received his eternal reward on Saturday, January 11, 2020 at 7:15 PM.

Dad was never a pastor, but he demonstrated the gospel through a life of servanthood. He was kind, compassionate, patient, and long suffering. Everything that I have in the way of honesty, character, integrity, work ethic, and parenthood I received from my Dad. He was always a man of few words, but his actions were my teacher. For my entire life I have been striving to be the man he was, yet I still seem to fall short.

Our family has been through our share of tragedy, but my Dad was the anchor that held us together. He was a model of Godliness, love, strength, and character. I will always strive to emulate the example he lived. I miss him every day.

Dedication

TEN REASONS WHY

Pastors are in Danger

JEFF WOLF

Foreword

Imagine interviewing for your dream job. You have prepared your whole life for this moment. You have spent money on education, you've served and paid your dues. You're ready for your hard work to pay off. The day comes that you are chosen above all other candidates. You're the one! With great excitement, you accept the position, and shortly thereafter receive the following letter.

"Welcome to your new house; it is a benefit of your new position and was built especially for you. We hope that you will enjoy many years of happiness here, and make precious memories with your family. Before you move in, there are a few little things we think you should know. Your new house is made of glass. You will be watched, day in and day out; every move you make will be scrutinized and you will rarely have privacy. In the center of this house is a pedestal for you to sit on. You will be expected to stay on that pedestal and never come off.

You will be at the beck and call of many people. You will often be expected to drop everything to tend to the needs of others,

Introduction

The pastorate is one of the most fulfilling and rewarding ministries one can have. It's an exclusive fraternity of men and women who have answered a call for which they can never be fully prepared. They gladly leave all behind to answer that call, without regard for their own aspirations, often not knowing where it will take them or what it will pay. Pastors put themselves in the hands of God to be sustained and run to their parish like a fireman running toward a flame, excited to have been chosen for such a holy and noble cause. There's nothing like it. I am grateful to have been called, "pastor".

As with any important undertaking, there are risks. There is danger. No one knew the danger of ministry like the Apostle Paul. Paul was a circuit preacher, making his rounds to the churches which he had planted throughout Asia Minor. When he was not with the saints physically, he wrote them letters (now comprising a large part of the New Testament). One such letter was to the church in Corinth. Of the many things he addressed in the letter was the issue of the boasting of his adversaries. It triggers the passage found in 2 Corinthians 11:23-28.

"I have worked much harder, been in prison more frequently, been flogged more severely, and been exposed to death again and again. Five times I received from the Jews the forty lashes minus one. Three times I was beaten with rods, once I was pelted with stones, three times I was shipwrecked, I spent a night and a day in the open sea, I have been constantly on the move. I have been in danger from rivers, in danger from bandits, in danger from my fellow Jews, in danger from Gentiles; in danger in the city, in danger in the country, in danger at sea; and in danger from false believers. I have labored and toiled and have often gone without sleep; I have known hunger and thirst and have often gone without food; I have been cold and naked. Besides everything else, I face daily the pressure of my concern for all the churches." (NIV)

Paul's pedigree was that of a Roman citizen, born a Jew of the tribe of Benjamin. He was second generation Pharisee and studied under Gamaliel, a doctor of Jewish law. He was an impressive man. Yet, when confronted with the boasting of false teachers who were coming to present to the Corinthians a different way to salvation, Paul responded in a unique way. Rather than rehearse his triumphs, he said, *"If I must boast, I will boast of the things that show my weakness." (2 Corinthians 11:30 NIV)*

Our weaknesses are something we are seldom willing to talk about, much less boast of. In fact, we are predisposed to hide our weaknesses behind a mask of perfection. We feel we dare not reveal our weaknesses for fear of our public persona or reputation being tarnished by the notion we are actually human. The truth is we *are* human. I left out verse 29 to insert it here. In spite of his impressive resume, this Apostle extraordinaire said, "Who is weak, and I do not feel weak? Who is led into sin, and I do not inwardly burn?" (NIV). Paul has exposed his humanity to his congregation to reinforce his identification with their daily struggles.

David is another Biblical leader that allowed us to see his humanity. In 1 Samuel 21, he is captured by the Philistines as he flees from an angry and jealous King Saul. Verse 12 tell us David was "very much afraid of Achish king of Gath." (NIV). He had been recognized by the Philistines and feigned insanity to disguise himself and was subsequently released. David remembered his experience with a song in which he wrote, "When I am afraid, I put my trust in you." (Psalm 56:3 NIV).

Look at the prophet Elijah. In 1 Kings 18, he presided over a showdown with the prophets of Baal. He witnessed the unimpeachable power of Jehovah, Who sent fire upon the sacrifice. Elijah ordered the prophets of Baal slain, and prophesied rain after a three-and-a-half year period of draught and famine. If that wasn't enough, He told King Ahab to mount his chariot and head for home before the rain stopped him, then outran Ahab's chariot back to Jezreel under the power of the Spirit. God used Elijah in a very powerful way that day. But something happened in chapter 19. King Ahab told Jezebel that Elijah killed all the prophets of Baal and she responded with a threat: you'll be dead by this time tomorrow. This mighty man of God, this prophet who called fire down from Heaven, called rain out of the clouds, and outran a king's chariot, immediately forgot who he was and cowered in fear. Verse 3 says, "Elijah was afraid and ran for his life." (NIV)

These three leaders, God's men, are revealed in their raw humanity in the scripture. The message to us is that even great and noble leaders are not immune from the human response to danger.

Let's talk about danger. It is common in our society. I spent two decades in law enforcement. Every time I left the house in uniform, I was in danger. Not just danger of being physically injured or killed, but danger of lawsuit, danger of emotional or mental trauma, danger of the effects of P.T.S.D., etc. For first responders, such danger is just another day at the office. It didn't really cross my mind most days.

Likewise, many other professions involve some element of danger, including ministry. What? Yes. Pastors are in danger. The Apostle Paul uses the word "danger" eight times in the above passage. Now, granted, he experienced persecution and peril unlike anything we've ever known. His final thought, however, was that all of that danger was in addition to the daily pressure of his pastoral concern. Having spent my adult life in ministry, I can closely relate to that thought.

I realize this concept may be difficult to understand if you've never walked in a pastor's shoes. After all, every time you see your pastor, they probably shake your hand or give you a hug with a bright smile on their face and, as they speak, you can feel the warmth and concern radiating from their words, right? How could a pastor's job be dangerous? Well, there's a difference between the pastor you see and the pastor you don't. What I mean by that is, the pastor you see is the one who is often making a concerted effort to hide their own pain and suffering in order to focus on you. The pastor you don't see is the pastor that is well acquainted with their humanity, personality flaws, weaknesses, and failures, and sometimes wonders if they're being the pastor you need them to be. While you may be willing to let your pastor see your weaknesses, your pastor may not always be willing to do the same. It's not because they have something to hide, but because they are selfless and often suppress their own feelings to ministers to others.

Here's where you ask the question. What dangers do pastors face? I'm glad you asked! I'm going to give you ten reasons your pastor is in danger, some staggering feedback to support this information, some practical takeaways, and show you how to cover them in prayer accordingly.

I asked pastors and ministry leaders to respond to an anonymous inventory of their ministry experience. The respondents were presented with a series of statements and asked to respond to each with one of three answers: agree, undecided, or disagree. It is important to note that this was not conducted as a scientific poll, and the results are not intended to represent a sample of likely pastors. It is also of note that the respondents are pastors who are likely sensing fatigue and/or an impending burnout in their lives, and believe they are at risk. Therefore, the results may be skewed, however, they are intended to bring focus to the dangers that pastors face and create a guide to direct us in caring and praying for those on the front lines of ministry.

In the pages that follow, I'm going to share those responses and uncover some things that will help you identify with the humanity of the pastorate. I want you to walk away with an appreciation and compassion for pastors with an understanding you've never had.

Before we jump in, I will add a disclaimer. Not all pastors are struggling. However, there are bleeding shepherds who have reached out anonymously to be honest about their struggle. We can't dismiss them. We must get under their arms and hold them up.

1
Because They Have Moments of Weakness.

Pastors are in danger because they have moments of weakness. Since I've used Paul as a poster child, let's look at 2 Corinthians 12: 5-10:

"I will not boast about myself, except about my weaknesses. Even if I should choose to boast, I would not be a fool, because I would be speaking the truth. But I refrain, so no one will think more of me than is warranted by what I do or say, or because of these surpassingly great revelations. Therefore, in order to keep me from becoming conceited, I was given a thorn in my flesh, a messenger of Satan, to torment me. Three times I pleaded with the Lord to take it away from me. But he said to me, "My grace is sufficient for you, for my power is made perfect in weakness." Therefore I will boast all the more gladly about my weaknesses, so that Christ's power may rest on me. That is why, for Christ's sake, I delight in weaknesses, in insults, in hardships, in persecutions, in difficulties. For when I am weak, then I am strong." (NIV)

Most people believe that showing weakness is bad. Hence old sayings like, "Never let 'em see you sweat", or "Pain is weakness leaving the body". If you have a weakness there must be something wrong with you, right? Wrong. According to Paul, the exact opposite is true.

As believers, we live by Kingdom principles which are much different from human principles. Paul writes that Kingdom principles say, God's power is made perfect in my weakness, His grace is sufficient, and I'm strongest when I'm at my weakest. Therefore, if I'm going to boast about something, it should be my weaknesses because therein is God glorified.

Paul even goes so far as to say that, for these reasons, he *delights* in weaknesses. The word Paul uses is *eudokéō,* which means to be well pleased.[1] How can Paul be *pleased* about his weaknesses? I believe the central theme of his letter is not the weakness, but the inability of the weakness to weaken him. Read that again. Being pleased or delighted with your weaknesses is to acknowledge that your source of strength is the response of the omnipotent God to your frail humanity. The weaker I am, the stronger He becomes through me.

Your pastor has moments of weakness, but doesn't always see their weakness through the lens of 2 Corinthians 12. I don't recall ever hearing a pastor boast of their weaknesses. In fact, most pastors don't boast at all. It is quite the opposite.

67% OF RESPONDING PASTORS SAY THEY ARE CONSTANTLY CRITICAL OF THEMSELVES.

There's a difference between introspection and being constantly critical of oneself. Introspection is what David was doing when he wrote Psalm 139:23-24.

"Search me, God, and know my heart; test me and know my anxious thoughts. See if there is any offensive way in me, and lead me in the way everlasting." (NIV)

Being constantly critical is pronouncing negative judgment upon oneself. It may come from feelings of inadequacy, the notion that I'm not good enough, I'm not doing enough, or I should've done better. It is natural to be your own worst critic, but to be constantly critical of yourself is most likely the result of allowing outside negative criticism to get the best of you.

I can closely relate to this response. I'm somewhat of a perfectionist and workaholic. Regardless of how hard I worked on something, and how good it was, I still felt it wasn't good enough. What a congregation sees as a quality work and ministry product from their pastor, that pastor may be beating himself up over it. "I'm not good enough. I'm not doing enough, I should've done better."

How does one counteract constant negative self criticism? Do what David did. Practice prayerful introspection and give it to the Lord. He will show you where you need to improve.

25% OF RESPONDING PASTORS SAY THEY WOULD QUIT IF THEY COULD.

When a pastor believes they are not strong enough to carry out the work of ministry, that their weaknesses are too great to be effective, that they are not worthy, they will think about quitting. I believe, if we were being honest, most pastors could say they've *thought* about it at least once in their career. Hasn't everyone had a bad enough day that they had a thought about quitting, at least once? There's nothing abnormal about that, right?

This is different. When a pastor says, "I would quit if I could", they've given it some serious thought. They've weighed the pros and cons. They've looked at their budget. They have taken all things into consideration and decided, for whatever reason, they just can't do it. "I would quit if I could, but I just can't."

This is something that a pastor would keep close. To admit that quitting is being considered as an option, even to a close and trusted friend, would expose our weaknesses. Remember, we don't expose our weaknesses, let alone delight in them.

When a pastor gets to this point, they are in serious danger. They have allowed their weaknesses to discourage them. They have allowed the devil to convince them they are unable to go on walking in their calling. This pastor could do one of several things. Firstly, they could quit altogether. Secondly, they could leave and pastor another church. Thirdly, they could keep plugging away until burnout sets in. In my opinion, none of these options is ideal if the underlying issues aren't dealt with.

So, what can we do? Seek understanding and seek the face of God on their behalf.

TAKEAWAY

You will likely not know if or when your pastor is struggling. However, every pastor would benefit from their congregation having a better understanding of what they're up against. Here is what I would want my congregation to know.

Give your pastor permission to be human. Understand that they have weaknesses just like everyone else, and are hyper-aware of them. Understand that, because of those weaknesses, your pastor is likely more critical of themselves than anyone else could ever be. Understand that they are called, chosen, and doing the best they can to minister in the volatile environment within which they are placed. Understand that many have quit or considered quitting under the pressure, but your pastor is still on the wall.

Understand that your pastor's job description is vast and complicated, but includes 2 Timothy 4:2:

"Preach the word; be prepared in season and out of season; correct, rebuke and encourage--with great patience and careful instruction." (NIV)

That one sentence is a mouthful all by itself. At the risk of kicking into expository preaching mode, I want to point out one phrase: in season and out of season. Paul uses the words, *eukairós* and *akairós*, meaning *conveniently* and *inopportunely*, respectively.[2] Timothy's instructions were this: you will work when it's convenient and you will work when it's not.

Understand that ministry is a 24/7 calling. It's not always easy, and its not always pleasant, but your pastor is giving it 100%. Pray for your pastor.

PRAYER FOR STRENGTH

Heavenly Father, I pray strength over my pastor. I acknowledge that they are human and faces life's dilemmas as anyone else. I understand that they have moments of weakness and gets discouraged. I, therefore, cover my pastor in prayer.

I petition you, Lord, in my pastor's weakness, that you would allow your power to be made perfect; that in that weakness you will impart Your strength. I speak joy over my pastor, calling You to Your Word that declares, "The joy of the Lord is my strength!" May the man/woman of God be sustained by Your Divine strength.

I cancel every assignment of the devil against my pastor that would attempt to exploit them in their weakness. Silence the lies of the enemy that would declare inadequacy over their life and ministry.

I prophesy strength and courage over my pastor, and declare that no weapon formed against them will prosper. Amen!

2
Because They Deal With Conflict.

Pastors are in danger because they deal with conflict. As you can tell by now, the letters of the Apostle Paul have become the sandbox from which I support this topic. Paul was the master pastor; consider his instructions to his young protégé in 2 Timothy 2:23-25:

> "Don't have anything to do with foolish and stupid arguments, because you know they produce quarrels. And the Lord's servant must not be quarrelsome but must be kind to everyone, able to teach, not resentful. Opponents must be gently instructed, in the hope that God will grant them repentance leading them to a knowledge of the truth." (NIV)

Conflict is as American as apple pie and baseball. There is conflict in the home, conflict in the workplace, conflict in the marketplace, conflict in the city, conflict in the country, conflict in the government; if you put two people on a boat in the middle of the ocean, they will argue about which way to row. Where two or more are gathered there will be conflict, including within the body of Christ. Who finds themselves in the middle of conflict? Pastors.

Contextually, Paul's second letter to Timothy was written during a time when believers were in conflict about doctrine. Paul often warns of false teachers and those coming to present a "different gospel" (2 Corinthians 11:4). Paul wants to make sure Timothy stays focused and doesn't get in the middle of "stupid and foolish arguments."

Have you ever had to hide your emotions? Perhaps the better question is, how many times a day do you have to hide your emotions? Paul is basically telling Timothy, "You know these arguments are stupid and lead to quarrels, but you can't tell them that. You have to hide your natural human emotions and be a gentle and kind mediator.

Have you ever found yourself in the middle of a conflict and wanted to give someone a piece of your mind? So has your pastor. The calling of ministry doesn't magically remove someone's human reactions and emotions. There have been times I wanted to react like Nehemiah when he said, "I rebuked them and called curses down on them. I beat some of the men and pulled out their hair..." (Nehemiah 13:25 NIV). Pastors can't act that way; it's not kind or gentle, and may land you in jail. However, I believe most pastors can identify with Nehemiah's anger when it comes to stupid arguments and quarrels in the church.

Conflict is the pulling of two forces in opposite directions. Ideally, conflict either results in resolution or separation. Resolution often requires a mediator, someone who can objectively pull two opposing forces together and help them compromise and find common ground. That seems like what Pastor Timothy is instructed to do.

50% OF RESPONDING PASTORS SAY THEIR STRESS LEVEL IS HIGH.

Conflict resolution in the 21st century has become much more complicated. Rather than seeking to resolve a conflict, people breed conflict. How does that happen? Social media.

In simpler times, you had to look someone in the eye, or talk to them and either fight it out or argue it out. Social media, however, has made conflict so much more convenient. Now, you can start trouble with a few key strokes from the privacy and comfort of your own home. Many people have made a sport of disagreeing with others on social media. According to an article on Forbes.com, a survey found that 20% of people below the age of 38 said they were likely to get into an argument online. The same article quotes Jim Purtilo, associate professor in the computer science department at the University of Maryland, as saying, "Discussion at a distance can quickly spiral out of control in ways that would never happen in face-to-face exchanges."[3] It's almost as if people can't help themselves.

Isn't it amazing how Paul's warning to Timothy is still so immediately relevant, two centuries later? "Don't have anything to do with foolish and stupid arguments." (2 Tim 2:23 NIV). If I were going to publish "Wolf's Unauthorized Translation" (WUT), I would write that verse a little differently. It would say something like, "Pastor Tim, don't take the bait when someone pushes your buttons, especially online."

On one hand, social media is a powerful tool and, if leveraged properly, can enhance your ministry. During the recent pandemic, when people couldn't go to church they turned to social media for the Word. Ministries all over the world flooded social media with live-stream worship; it was powerful. We are using it to proclaim the Gospel to the nations!

On the other hand, social media can be extremely toxic and can even steal your peace. I believe it has become a major source of stress for pastors. There's nothing like scrolling your feed and finding out one of your congregants has a beef with you, and you seem to be the last one to know about it.

Conflict is often directed at pastors themselves. I never went looking for a conflict, but it always seemed to find me. Like the time someone sent me a disapproving e-mail. I was a very young pastor and didn't know any better; I responded to the e-mail. I arrived at the church on the following Sunday to discover my e-mail had been doctored, printed, and passed out to members of the congregation. Fool me once, shame on you.

America has become so conflict driven that, any more, you have to be careful what you say, post, or even believe. This goes double for pastors. If I may borrow a phrase from the Miranda Warning, anything pastors say can and usually will be used against them. I used to think that if I stuck to scripture I'd be safe, but even drawing certain biblical lines will make you controversial, and thereby spark conflict.

Perhaps you've heard the term, "cancel culture." In a nutshell, cancel culture is targeting someone, usually on social media, for making a statement or taking a stand that is found to be offensive, for the purpose of weakening their influence.

Cancel culture has become the social media court of disciplinary action against those whose message is offensive to someone. That someone then recruits an offended mob, aiming to "cancel" the person who has spoken offensively. The New York Times defined cancel culture as, "depriving people of a platform."[4]

Cancel culture amounts to this: anyone with a beef, if they get a big enough mob, can attack anyone with no accountability and no consequences. It's a bully tactic. Those who engage in cancel campaigns use buzz phrases, describing the words of someone with an opposing view as, "hurtful and intolerant", or "culturally insensitive".

Pastors have been victims of cancel culture before the term was ever officially coined; It is cancel culture when a churchgoer doesn't like what their pastor says, so they began to sew discord and division in the body. It is cancel culture when someone is offended by the preaching of the truth, and leave the church to find someone who will scratch their itching ears. Now we have a name for it. Cancel culture.

Before you write this off as irrelevant to people of faith, listen to this story.

In early summer of 2020, Pastor Chris Hodges of Church of the Highlands, in Birmingham, Alabama was the victim of cancel culture. Church of the Highlands is a large church and is known for its outreach ministries. Pastor Hodges was targeted by a local English teacher, who did not attend the church, who decided to catalogue the pastor's likes on social media and share them with the press. She began a smear campaign that resulted in the Birmingham Board of Education cancelling the church's lease on 2 local schools, effectively ending two of its worship venues. In addition, the church's Christ Health Clinic was banned from operating, and the church was banned from ministering in the city's public housing communities.[5]

Pastor Hodges didn't make a controversial statement. He didn't preach something that offended someone. He didn't take a hard line on a particular doctrine. He was targeted simply for his "likes" on what was viewed as conservative social media content.

The thought that a pastor's ministries could be interrupted and a platform taken away because of a manufactured conflict based on his passive opinions is startling. People are literally looking for reasons to stir the pot and pastors are not untouched by this cancel culture.

TAKEAWAY

Pastors are in danger because they often deal with conflict. Those conflicts can be as minor as a disagreement between two church leaders, or as major as a conflict that arises out of public persecution of the pastor himself, threatening his ministry. Conflicts come in all shapes and sizes. Regardless of who you are, there's surely a conflict with your name on it.

Why is it dangerous? Because, pastors are big targets of conflict, and it causes severe stress. We weren't built to endure severe and sustained stress. Its easy to go weeks and even months and allow stress to go unchecked. It can develop into unhealthy coping mechanisms as well. The Mayo Clinic says, "Stress that's left unchecked can contribute to many health problems, such as high blood pressure, heart disease, obesity and diabetes."[6]

One of the greatest commodities for a pastor is peace. Peace from the noise. Peace from the storm. Peace from the conflict. Peace from the stress. Pastors aren't super human, they need to be encouraged just like anyone else. I challenge you to be the encourager that your pastor may need today.

"Anxiety weighs down the heart but a kind word cheers it up." (Proverbs 12:25 NIV)

PRAYER FOR PEACE

Lord, today I intercede on behalf of my pastor. When the enemy targets them, place a shield of protection about them. When they are discouraged, let the wind of Your presence fill the room and comfort their heart and mind.

Father, give my pastor strength to stand steadfast when adversity arrises, and give them words of wisdom and grace when conflict surfaces. May you do for my pastor as you did for King David, prepare a table for them in the presence of the enemy.

Now, Lord, may Your peace that passes all understanding cover my pastor like a blanket. May Your peace dominate the noise around them so that they may find You in the quite place. May Your peace take the edge off of the sharp words spoken against them that they might find rest from the conflict. May Your peace rule their heart and mind continually, as they seek to know Your heart and speak Your words.

Hide my pastor in the cleft of the rock, so that they may be shielded from the storm. Thank you, Lord for the shepherd you have sent to watch the flock of God. I pray this in Jesus' name. Amen!

3
Because They Often Feel Lonely.

Pastors are in danger because they often feel lonely. I find it challenging to offer you an explanation for leadership loneliness. If you've never been in a leadership position, such as that of a pastor, it is not easily understood. The best, and most eloquent, description I've read is in A.W. Tozer's book, *The Radical Cross*.

> "The man who has passed on into the divine presence in actual inner experience will not find many who understand him. A certain amount of social fellowship will of course be his as he mingles with religious persons in the regular activities of the church, but true spiritual fellowship will be hard to find. But he should not expect things to be otherwise. After all, he is a stranger and a pilgrim, and the journey he takes is not on his feet but in his heart. He walks with God in the garden of his own soul—and who but God can walk there with him?"[7]

67% OF RESPONDING PASTORS SAY THEY OFTEN FEEL LONELY.

Loneliness in pastoral leadership is not about spiritual superiority. It's about a sense of calling. Those who have answered that call have entered into a lifelong commitment from which they can never resign. A calling to ministry is nothing short of an epiphany. I didn't physically see Jesus appear before me, but I heard His Words so clearly that it removed all doubt. I have been called to ministry. To understand, you have to have shared a similar experience.

Pastors understand pastors, but there is often a relational gap between pastors. Unless they are communicating with each other on a regular basis, they have no relational outlet to help them deal with the issues only pastors understand.

As I said, it's not an issue of superiority; your pastor is not better than you. It's an issue of lateral understanding. If you've never walked in a pastor's shoes, you can't possibly understand the demands of their role. It's not like being a business owner, or a CEO, etc. Ministry is something to which there is no reference of comparison. Therefore, pastors often experience loneliness.

The old adage, "It's lonely at the top," is certainly true.

58% OF RESPONDING PASTORS SAY THEY HAVE NO CLOSE FRIENDS.

We have to humanize pastors. I am no less human than one who is on the other side of the sermon. I need meaningful friendships in my life, just like anyone else. While I have many ministry colleagues, I have traditionally had a very small circle of friends. I believe most pastors can relate.

I think you would agree; friends are necessary. Why do we need friends? Consider an answer found in 1 Samuel 23:26.

> "And Saul's son Jonathan went to David at Horesh and helped him find strength in God." (NIV)

There is no better illustration of true earthly friendship found in all of scripture, than that of David and Jonathan. There couldn't have been two more different people than the two of them. Jonathan was a prince. David was a shepherd boy. Yet, God knit them together as friends.

> *"After David had finished talking with Saul, Jonathan became one in spirit with David, and he loved him as himself. From that day Saul kept David with him and did not let him return home to his family. And Jonathan made a covenant with David because he loved him as himself. Jonathan took off the robe he was wearing and gave it to David, along with his tunic, and even his sword, his bow and his belt."* (1 Samuel 18:1-4 NIV)

Just like this shepherd-boy-turned-king, I've often found myself needing a friend to help me find strength in God. By God's grace, I've been blessed with just such friends.

I have three close friends, all three of whom are pastors. I have always been able to talk to them about anything I was going through, with no judgment or explanation, because they understand. I'm thankful for those three men, but our ministry assignments have always separated us geographically. We frequently exchange phone calls or text messages, and, although we don't have many opportunities to get together, we've remained close through the years. Outside of that, I've had very few friendships in the pastorate.

You may be thinking, "wait a second. Doesn't a pastor have a congregation full of people with whom they can have friendships?" It's difficult to explain this without sounding exclusive, but the truth is, no. Pastor's do form friendships within their inner circle, and that circle comes from the remnant, usually leadership. However, that accounts for a very small portion of the people they pastor.

Here is the challenge; friendships between pastor and parishioner are unique. Imagine a shepherd appearing as if he is favoring a few of the sheep above the rest of the flock. Sheering is confrontational and can be unpleasant for the sheep, therefore, the shepherd may choose not to sheer those sheep as often as the others. When a sheep isn't sheered regularly, it can cause health problems. Or, the shepherd may not use his staff to correct those sheep like he does the others. Of course, I'm speaking metaphorically about the pastor's role of shepherd, and responsibility of providing leadership and correction for those to whom they minister. You get the picture.

For pastors, the line between parishioner and friend is very thin. In order for a pastor to have a healthy friendship within their inner circle, the pastor and the parishioner must both be able to stay on their respective sides of the line. It's dangerous for one to be too familiar with the other. Not everyone can walk that tightrope. The danger is found in losing that delicate balance and landing in the valley of betrayal.

75% OF RESPONDING PASTORS SAY THEY HAVE EXPERIENCED BETRAYAL IN THEIR INNER CIRCLE.

When pastors do form friendships among their congregants, some have reported that they experienced betrayal as a result. It's very easy for pastors to get close to those within their inner circle. This comes from working together, worshipping together, eating together, travelling together, etc. Multiply that factor by a pastor's longevity and the bonds of friendship can become very strong. These folks become like family. By virtue of their proximity, they observe a pastor in the best and worst of times. They are most likely to see a pastor's humanity. Because they are trusted, a pastor is not afraid to allow his humanity to peak through. Unfortunately, some people are not spiritually mature enough to handle a pastor's humanity.

When someone is capable of respecting the line between pastor and friend, everything is fine. But, what happens when someone takes advantage of that friendship? What happens when someone gets too comfortable and casual with their pastor? What happens when a pastor begins to feel that someone's friendship is conditioned upon their approval of his performance? This is where things get a little sticky, and the balance is lost.

Betrayal happens when someone you trust determines you no longer meet certain conditions, and they buy into something they've decided is more valuable to them than your friendship. You cannot be betrayed by an acquaintance; there is no investment involved. The investment factor is what makes betrayal so painful. Look at Psalm 41:9:

> *"Even my close friend, someone I trusted, one who shared my bread, has turned against me." (NIV).*

I learned this lesson the hard way. One day someone is your closest ally. The next day, you receive a text or social media message that they are leaving the church. It always made me feel betrayed. I trusted them. I let my hair down in front of them. I confided in them at times. I dedicated their children, visited their relatives in the hospital, buried their parents, expecting nothing in return. How can they just walk away like that?

It's really hard for a pastor not to take this personally. In my experience, I had to remind myself that investment into people is a Kingdom investment, and it will return to me with Kingdom dividends. Nonetheless, when one experiences a pattern of betrayal, it leads to trust issues.

83% OF RESPONDING PASTORS SAY THEY ARE HESITANT TO TRUST PEOPLE.

This is the next exit off the highway. Lack of trust doesn't happen over night. It is caused by a pattern of betrayal that leads to estrangement from people whom were once trusted friends.[8] This is difficult territory for a pastor; it's difficult to lead and minister to others when you have trust issues.

Here's what I know about pastors, they are good at internalizing. The ministry requires it. I suppose temporary internalization is necessary to maintain composure in difficult circumstances, and make decisions without involving emotion. Internalization is a defense mechanism in times of stress for many of us. However, just as prolonged stress can be harmful, so is a sustained response to stress.

Internalized emotions have to be expressed at some point. If not, those emotions build and compound, slowly metastasizing into other issues, such as low self-esteem, social isolation, loneliness, and even depression.[9] Everyone needs a trusted person or group of persons to whom they can express their emotions, vent, and confide in. When a pastor has trouble trusting people as a result of betrayal experiences, it can be a result of sustained internalization without a pressure release valve of meaningful friendships.

When we lack trust, we'll hold the wrong people accountable. If person "A" betrayed my trust, then a few months later, person "B" betrayed my trust, when person "C" comes along, they'll end up paying for sins they didn't commit (so to speak). When you don't trust people, you won't communicate, you won't confront issues, and worst of all, you won't invest in them. Pastor's cannot afford to relate to others through the lens of loneliness. It's dangerous.

The ultimate danger is the opportunity taken by the adversary to exploit loneliness and plant the seeds of temptation.

TAKEAWAY

Pastors are in danger because they often feel lonely. Many pastors feel lonely because they don't have many close friendships. They don't have close friendships because they've experienced betrayal in their inner circle and hesitate to trust people. I draw this conclusion out of my own personal experience.

Unfortunately, I don't believe betrayal can be prevented. If Jesus was betrayed, then so will I be. The question then becomes, what can we do to support our pastors in this regard? First and foremost, pray that God will send friends into your pastor's life from outside the church, that they can trust, talk to, confide in, and lean on.

Secondly, be a friend, a genuine friend, a friend that expects nothing in return. Do simple things like sending a text just to say, "Pastor, I'm thinking about you and praying for you today." Get your pastor a $5 gift card to their favorite coffee place with a note just to say, "Pastor, you're important and essential to our family. Have a coffee on us!" It doesn't take much. Small gestures over time are far more meaningful (in my humble opinion) than a large one-time gesture.

Love on your pastor. I promise it will not go unnoticed, and it will boost their confidence.

PRAYER FOR RELATIONSHIPS

Heavenly Father, thank you for my friends. You given them to me to share in my joys and comfort me in my sorrows. They have been there for me to lean on in times of weakness and loneliness. They have given me advice and moral support in times of decision. They have given me perspective when I couldn't see. They've often spoken to me the things I've needed to hear. I'm so thankful for Godly friends.

Lord, I pray that you will bless my pastor with those kinds of friendships; friends they can trust without fear of betrayal. Shield my pastor from feelings of loneliness. Bring healing to their heart from past betrayal. Thank You for Your protection from the hazards of ministry created by loneliness.

We declare Your Word, Lord, that promises You are a Friend that sticks closer than a brother. May my pastor walk in the peace and comfort that comes from knowing that You are near.

4
Because Sometimes They Don't Know What To Do.

Pastors are in danger because sometimes they don't know what to do. You're probably thinking, "But my pastor always knows what to do!"

If you've read *Restored*, you know I love military history. Here's a short history lesson. One of the turning points of World War 2 was the capture of a German U-boat and its enigma encoding machine by HMS Bulldog, a British Destroyer, in May of 1941. The Americans later captured another enigma from U-505. The machine encoded German messages into what amounted to gibberish before transmission. When the messages were received, they were decoded by the enigma. Capturing these devices essentially gave the Allies the ability to intercept and interpret German intelligence. Historians believe this may have shortened the war.[10]

The film *U-571* is loosely based upon this historic capture. In the film, the executive officer of an American submarine finds himself and a remnant of his crew aboard a captured German U-boat. The vessel is weak, the engines are damaged, his crew is tired and afraid, and he has never commanded a ship before. It's a dire situation, to say the least. When one of his crew members asks what his plan is, he replies, "I don't know."

In the next scene, the old, salty, battle hardened master chief gets the X.O. (now captain) alone and respectfully admonishes him,

"You're the skipper now, and the skipper always knows what to do whether he does or not. Don't you dare say what you said to the boys back there again, 'I don't know.' Those three words will kill a crew, dead as a depth charge. You're the skipper now, and the skipper always knows what to do whether he does or not."[11]

As a pastor, I have felt the pressure of being in difficult situations and not knowing what to do. This comes from being in situations you've never been in, have never prepared for, and have no experience or frame of reference to guide you. When I don't know what to do, I often feel like the directions I receive from the Lord are encrypted, like the messages sent by the German enigma. I find myself asking the Lord, "What are You trying to say to me?" I know you've been there as well. Guess what? So has your pastor.

42% OF RESPONDING PASTORS SAY THEY DON'T FEEL PROPERLY EQUIPPED FOR MINISTRY.

Four years of undergraduate studies, three years of seminary, and a doctorate of divinity will prepare you academically for ministry, but it won't prepare you for everything. Pastoral ministry is a complex, multifaceted, and painstaking lifestyle. While pastors look to scripture for guidance, there is no manual or how-to video for every twist and turn they will need to navigate. I wish there were; it would've made life a little easier.

Candidly, no one ever explained to me how to deal with confrontational church members, disgruntled board members, family conflicts within the church, power struggles between influential leaders, hecklers during the sermon, drunks who came in the office to beat me up because they thought I was the previous pastor (yes that actually happened), etc. There were times I had no idea what I was doing! I had to figure it out on my own with much prayer!

On-the-job experience, the school of hard knocks, whatever you want to call it, there are some things you don't learn until you have had the experience. For those things which cannot be learned academically, a pastor needs a mentor to walk with them on the journey. A mentor has been there and done that. They have already gained the knowledge and wisdom that comes from having been on the front lines. That wisdom is tried and tested and an invaluable resource.

Perhaps the best scriptural model of the mentoring relationship is given by the Apostle Paul. In several places, Paul makes it clear that he wants believers to emulate his example.

"Follow my example, as I follow the example of Christ." (1 Corinthians 11:1 NIV)

"Whatever you have learned or received or heard from me, or seen in me—put it into practice." (Philippians 4:9 NIV)

"For you yourselves know how you ought to follow our example." (1 Thessalonians 3:7 NIV)

Mentoring relationships provide accountability, confidence, and safety. Most pastors understand the concept of mentorship and have looked to their pastor or an elder minister for that guidance. Personally, I have emulated my pastor and others I've respected over the years. I don't think I would've have made it without them.

When cadets attend police academy for six months, graduate and become police officers, they aren't just given the keys to a police vehicle and told to go do the job. New officers undergo an average of six months of field training with a field training officer (FTO).

From my experience on both sides of that relationship, I can tell you there's a gap between classroom training and what actually happens on the streets. The gap is inevitable because of the real world factor. No matter how many scenarios you go through in training, there are always variables in the real world you either can't duplicate or didn't plan for. For this reason, extensive field training is vital to the success of a police officer. In the first phase they *observe* the FTO. In the second phase they *assist* the FTO. In the third and final phase they *do the job* under the supervision of the FTO. In each phase, the trainee is being evaluated by the FTO. Once the FTO is satisfied with the trainee's performance, he recommends they be released from field training.

Even after six months of police academy and six more months of field training, most police officers are scared to death the first time they patrol on their own. Why? Because, despite all the time spent preparing to do the job, they will encounter situations they were not prepared for.

42% OF RESPONDING PASTORS SAY THEY DO NOT HAVE SOMEONE THEY CONSIDER A MENTOR.

Not all pastors have had the benefit of field training. I was one of those pastors. I graduated from college, spent almost five years as an itinerate preacher, then was appointed to my first pastorate at the ripe young age of 25. I knew how to preach, but I had no idea how to pastor! I was just thrown into the deep end of the pool and expected to swim. There was a serious gap between academic training and what happened in the real world. There were moments when I looked back and said something like, "I didn't see that coming!" Many other pastors have had the same experience. It's quite inevitable.

Let's talk about the danger. The danger is not found in not knowing what to do. It is found in not seeking the support and wisdom of someone who does, but instead trying to go it alone. Contrary to your belief, your pastor does not always know what to do, but you will probably never hear that admission cross their lips. Why? Because *"the skipper always knows what to do whether he does or not!"*

When I turn to scripture, I find a leader who not only admitted he didn't know what to do, but did so in the company of his followers. In 2 Chronicles 20, King Jehoshaphat and Judah were besieged by the armies of Ammon, Moab, and Mount Seir. When the king heard of it, he called Judah to fast and pray. When they gathered, he stood before them and prayed; at the end of his prayer he said this:

"For we have no power to face this vast army that is attacking us. We do not know what to do, but our eyes are on You." (2 Chronicles 20:12 NIV)

It's okay if you don't know what to do! It doesn't make you weak, ignorant, or afraid. It makes you dependent upon the Word of the Lord. If you've been called, you've been trained, and prepared for this moment, even if you don't know what to do, you are not fighting the battle alone. You see, after the King finished his prayer, the Spirit of the Lord came upon a young man named Jahaziel. He declared:

"This is what the Lord says to you: 'Do not be afraid or discouraged because of this vast army. For the battle is not yours, but God's... You will not have to fight this battle. Take up your posi-

tions; stand firm and see the deliverance the Lord will give you, Judah and Jerusalem. Do not be afraid; do not be discouraged. Go out to face them tomorrow, and the Lord will be with you.'"
(2 Chronicles 20:15, 17 NIV)

The pastor may be the skipper of the vessel, but The Lord is the Master of the sea.

TAKEAWAY

The ability to lead a congregation cannot be separated from a total dependence upon the Great Shepherd. Understand that your pastor has answered the call to bear a great undertaking for the Kingdom of God. Pastors are on the front line of the battle between righteousness and unrighteousness and, like King Jehoshaphat, sometimes have to tell the Lord, "I don't know what to do."

Understand that your pastor is as human as you are. They are not walking on the clouds, caught up in the Spirit twenty-four-seven, with an anointing of omniscience. They have to fast and pray and seek the face of God just like you do. Though you may never hear your pastor say, "I don't know what to do," know that they have their moments and need you to support and pray for them.

The most effective thing you can do is pray that God will grant wisdom to your pastor in times of uncertainty. The Apostle James provides a good template for that prayer.

> *"Consider it pure joy, my brothers and sisters, whenever you face trials of many kinds, because you know that the testing of your faith produces perseverance. Let perseverance finish its work so that you may be mature and complete, not lacking anything. If any of you lacks wisdom, you should ask God, who gives generously to all without finding fault, and it will be given to you." (James 1:2-5 NIV)*

PRAYER FOR WISDOM

Lord, you are the omniscient God, the Creator of Heaven and Earth, nothing escapes Your view. You see the end from the beginning, and every step of the journey in between. There is no path down which You will send us for which You have not strengthened us. Our dependence is upon only You!

Father, I petition you on behalf of my pastor, as well as men and women of God everywhere, that you would be an ever present help in the time of trouble. In seasons of uncertainty, speak to them and give them direction and guidance. Grant them wisdom, according to your Word, beyond their years and experience. Give them eyes to see what others cannot see, and insight into difficult situations. Give them discernment to uncover the snares of the devil as they lead Your people.

Lord, intersect my pastor's life with someone of experience, Godly wisdom, and understanding who will mentor and lead them. May they have an example to follow; someone to warn them of the steps that lead to trouble, and give them insight that comes from experience.

Thank you, Lord, for your anointing upon my pastor to lead and provide an example for me to follow.

5
Because They Have Trouble Sleeping.

Pastors are in danger because they have trouble sleeping. At least, I did. Often when I laid down at night, it felt like the mental flood gates opened and thoughts of everything that I needed to do, should've done, could've done, or shouldn't have done seemed to attack me ferociously. My mind was flooded as I thought and over thought the events of the day, or agonized over what was to come the next day.

Okay, I know not everyone is like me. But I believe there are many people who can't go to sleep at night because they can't shut off their brain. Many people have taken medication just to help them sleep at night, including me.

A study published in 2013 by the CDC's National Center for Health Statistics reports an estimated 50 to 70 million Americans suffer from sleep disorders or sleep deprivation. Only a third of Americans get the recommended 7 to 9 hours of sleep per night, and nearly 9 million adults take prescription sleep aids. [12]

58% OF RESPONDING PASTORS SAY THEY HAVE TROUBLE SLEEPING.

The struggle is real. Pastors are among a certain group of professionals who have trouble "turning off" what they do. Like law enforcement officers, for example. When I'm driving down the road in my truck and another vehicle approaches, I still occasionally catch myself reaching for the radar remote as if I were driving a police car, conducting speed enforcement. It's muscle memory. What's more, police officers are expected to be police officers, on or off duty, when they observe a crime being committed. Therefore, it's difficult to turn it on and off, just like pastors.

Pastors always have ministry on the brain. They are always brainstorming, thinking about new ways to do ministry, new sermon ideas, that family they haven't seen in church for a couple of weeks, those persons in the hospital, those phone calls they need to make, that business they need to handle, those bills that need to be paid. It's always there, seemingly impossible to escape. When I laid down at night to sleep, it became worse. I can't tell you how many nights I laid there looking at the ceiling, just me, the darkness and my brain going 100 miles per hour, reminding me of every deficiency in my life and ministry. It was exhausting.

It even happened on vacation. One night, I woke up out of a dead sleep, in a hotel room in Myrtle Beach, having an anxiety attack. I didn't know it was an anxiety attack; I thought it was a heart attack. It scared me so bad, I went to the emergency room. Strangely, the initial medical screening was normal. Then the doctor asked me, "Have you had any stress lately?" I wanted to laugh out loud and say, "How much time do you have, doc?" Of course I had stress! I was a pastor with issues that needed my attention. What in the world was I doing taking a vacation?

Your pastor may be struggling with this, as well. Sleep deprivation will break you down physically over time, if you don't get a handle on it.

75% OF RESPONDING PASTORS SAY THEY FEEL TIRED AND WORN OUT.

When does sleep deprivation become dangerous? Columbia University Department of Neurology reports that sleep deprivation over time can cause increased risk for depression and mental illness, increased risk for stroke, heart disease, and asthma attack, hallucinations and severe mood swings.[13]

Based upon my personal experience, research, and conversations with pastors, I believe many of them are in the danger zone because they aren't getting enough sleep. What about your pastor? Do you think they are having trouble? I would challenge you to ask them. If you get an answer in the affirmative, start praying for them in this area.

Sleep deprivation is one of the areas in which I personally suffered a great deal. Like others I've talked to, I became physically, emotionally, and mentally exhausted because of lack of sleep. The reason I believe this is so dangerous is because it is the fast track to burnout. I don't want to get ahead of myself, but I want you to understand, anything that could lead to burnout must be addressed immediately. That goes for everyone, not just pastors.

So, why are we specifically targeting this danger for pastors? Firstly, because pastors are my burden, and the Lord called me to create resources to help them. Secondly, because pastors are always awake during the storm, just like the skipper of a ship tossed at sea. It's not because they have to be, but because they feel responsible to be at the helm.

How can I address this issue without singling out the familiar story of Matthew 8:23-25?

> *"Then he got into the boat and his disciples followed him. Suddenly a furious storm came up on the lake, so that the waves swept over the boat. But Jesus was sleeping. The disciples went and woke him, saying, "Lord, save us! We're going to drown!"* (NIV)

Let me point out that the only reason the disciples got on the boat to begin with was because Jesus got on the boat. They were following Jesus. The only reason they became afraid when the waves swept over the boat is because they were not in control of the boat, and the man who *was* in control, was asleep.

The church is like that boat in Matthew chapter 8. Undertaking pastoral ministry is not something that is done lightly. It is done with much prayer and only after receiving the direction of the Lord. When I got on the "boat" as the pastor, it is because I followed Jesus onto the "boat." Somewhere in the storm I became afraid because what was happening around me was out of my control. Like those disciples, I would ask the Lord, "Don't you see the storm? Don't you care what is happening? Did you lead me out here to drown?" Meanwhile, Jesus was always in control and I didn't have to be. He was giving me the example that it's okay to rest in the storm.

So, why did I reach a place where I was so tired and worn out all the time? Why do so many other pastors share that sentiment? I believe it was because my sleep patterns were so irregular. Sustained over time, it took me to a place where I never had any energy, ambition, or motivation, and it adversely affected my health.

The bottom line is this: sleep is important. If you aren't getting it you will pay a high price in the long run. Pastors have a hard time sleeping during the storm. You need to be proactive in holding them accountable in this area. They'll initially resist this notion, but I promise they'll thank you later.

TAKEAWAY

Your pastor eats, sleeps, and breathes ministry. Okay, maybe not the sleep part, but I don't believe I've met a pastor who has trouble with eating and breathing. Sleep is just as important as the other two, but is neglected the most.

Sleep is a category of your time budget you will "borrow" from when you are overspending in other areas. I used a similar illustration in *Restored*. You only have twenty-four hours in a day. On average, you need eight of those for work and eight more for sleep. That leaves you with eight to use for commutes, meals, family time, household tasks, reading, TV, and everything else.

If you work overtime, you have to cut into another category of your time bank (you can't make more time). If you binge watch your favorite show, you'll have to make up for it in another category of your time bank. If you do more work from home, you'll have to compensate from somewhere else in your schedule. Sleep is always the category that suffers, hands down.

This is dangerous and needs to be fixed right away! Your pastor can't afford to wait. You can be an advocate to help them take care of themselves. It may be as simple as sending them a quick text to say, "Hey Pastor, had you on my mind today. May I ask, are you getting enough sleep?" It may open the door to a conversation your pastor needs to have. It just may save a life and ministry.

PRAYER FOR REST

Lord, I thank You that Your word says:

"When you lie down, you will not be afraid; when you lie down, your sleep will be sweet." (Proverbs 3:24 NIV)

"In peace I will lie down and sleep, for you alone, LORD, make me dwell in safety." (Psalm 4:8 NV)

I pray rest over my pastor. I ask you to shield their mind with peace and assurance, and drown out the noise of stress and strife with Your word. Father I claim the promises of rest for my pastor, body, mind, and spirit. May they experience the restoration and rejuvenation that comes from a peaceful night's sleep. May they be full of life and energy, anointed with the physical strength to carry out the works that You have placed in their hands.

In Jesus' name, I come against fear, anxiety, worry, obsessive thoughts and every other weapon the adversary tries to use to steal restful sleep from my pastor. I ask you to silence the voices of criticism that echo in the mind and every other distraction that delays sleep.

I thank you for the transformation in my pastor's life that will come with this answered prayer.

6
Because They Are Bleeding.

Pastors are in danger because they are bleeding. In Matthew, Jesus applies a prophecy of Zechariah to Himself.

> "Then Jesus told them, "This very night you will all fall away on account of me, for it is written: 'I will strike the shepherd, and the sheep of the flock will be scattered.'" (Matthew 26:31 NIV)

He is referencing Zechariah 13:7, foretelling the betrayal of his disciples that very night and His physical suffering that will follow. Jesus, the Great Shepherd, was about to bleed for all humanity.

Scripture also gives the title of "shepherd" to pastors, while referring to Jesus as the *Chief Shepherd* in 1 Peter 5:2-4.

> "Be shepherds of God's flock that is under your care, watching over them—not because you must, but because you are willing, as God wants you to be; not pursuing dishonest gain, but eager to serve; not lording it over those entrusted to you, but being examples to the flock. And when the Chief Shepherd appears, you will receive the crown of glory that will never fade away." (NIV)

A pastor as shepherd also bleeds, but the wounds are mental and emotional and often created from within the flock. The thing about those kinds of wounds is they are invisible. Initially, the only person who knows a pastor is bleeding is the pastor himself.

58% OF RESPONDING PASTORS SAY THEY HAVE EXPERIENCED A TRAUMATIC EVENT IN THE LAST YEAR.

A traumatic event, for our purposes, is described in *Restored*. "Trauma is an emotional response to a negative event. There are multiple events that can have a negative mental and emotional impact on a pastor. A congregation split, the loss of an influential family, financial stress, negative criticism on social media, a confrontation, rejection, an attack on your integrity or your family, exposure to tragedy alongside members, just to name a few. Pastors regularly suffer from a combination of those issues, rather than just one. It is common for pastors to live under sustained pressure as a result of these negative events, and the pressure is crushing. All of that is in addition to any trauma the pastor has experienced in his personal life or family."[14]

When people, including pastors, experience trauma it causes a wound that hurts and bleeds. It is difficult for shepherds to tend to the flock when they are bleeding, because the pain of their own wound instinctively causes their focus to turn inward. Even the most caring, loving, selfless person you know, when they are sick, will be forced to focus on themselves to get well.

Notice, I said its difficult, not impossible. I've known folks that will care for others even in the midst of their own pain. I consider them to be next to sainthood. It is my experience that most pastors will also ignore their own pain to minister to others. This is very noble, but unsustainable. Eventually, the bleeding has to be addressed.

Please understand, I'm not pulling this information out of a hat; I'm giving you the benefit of my own experience. I can speak with authority in this area, being a recovered bleeding shepherd. That said, if your pastor is bleeding and consistently ignores his own pain, you will eventually see signs.

58% OF RESPONDING PASTORS SAY THE DON'T WANT TO BE AROUND PEOPLE.

As a reminder, these respondents are not a sampling of random pastors, but likely those who are already experiencing signs and symptoms of burn out. Please don't misunderstand the basis for this statistic and assume your pastor doesn't want to be around you if they are bleeding; that's not what I'm saying. What I *am* saying is that this is a sign that a pastor has suppressed their own pain for so long that it is beginning to spill over and they don't realize it. Just like a sponge, they have absorbed so much that they are saturated and begin dripping.

Not wanting to be around people was one of the first signs of my burn out. I will add a disclaimer with regard to my own experience; I'm naturally an extreme introvert who has to work hard on my social presence. This introvert reached a point, however, where I wasn't willing to make myself be social anymore. This isn't about being antisocial or not liking people. It's about isolation.

Isolation is dangerous. God did not create us to be isolated, but to commune and fellowship together.

> "Not giving up meeting together, as some are in the habit of doing, but encouraging one another--and all the more as you see the Day approaching." (Hebrews 10:25 NIV)

We often emphasize the first sentence of this verse, but zero in on one of the key reasons we are to meet together: to encourage one another.

"Even so the body is not made up of one part but of many." (1 Corinthians 12:14 NIV)

Further, the Apostle Paul uses the illustration of the body. We are all members of one body. When a member is missing, the body is not complete. It is no wonder the adversary plots and schemes to sew division and separation in the body. A dismembered body is a disadvantaged body.

When a pastor stops seeking fellowship with people, they are headed in the direction of isolation.

"Whoever isolates himself seeks his own desire; he breaks out against all sound judgment." (Proverbs 18:1 ESV)

Isolation is a defense mechanism used by people in pain (this is not to be confused with "isolation of affect" which is a psychological defense mechanism). It is the notion that if I stay away from people, I won't be hurt anymore or, If I stay to myself, I can take care of myself. It's not a sign of selfishness but rather self-preservation.

I'm the type of person who is unable to fake an emotion. In other words, if I'm unhappy or angry about something, I have a very difficult time hiding it, and replacing it with a more socially pleasant emotion. For instance, if I am upset about something, I hesitate to be around people because I will generally be expected to hide my feelings and appear happy. Since I'm terrible at faking it, I would just rather be alone until the negative emotion is over. But, what if the negative emotion doesn't end? What if my wound and subsequent pain has become so severe that it continues indefinitely? Then my desire to be alone turns into a pattern of isolation.

Pastors can't minister to others from a place of isolation. By virtue of their calling, they have to be out front. That's why a bleeding shepherd will eventually bleed through their clothes, so to speak, if their wound is not cared for. Isolation from people is a sign of that bleeding. If the bleeding isn't stopped, it can become something more dangerous.

58% OF RESPONDING PASTORS SAY THEY ARE EMOTIONALLY DETACHED.

"Detachment can best be described as a process of letting go."[15] I cannot write this without recalling my own experience. At a certain point, I had hurt so severely for so long that I had emotionally checked out. To prevent further pain I adopted an "I don't care" mentality. To stop caring is to stop allowing people and things to cause further pain. Detachment is a symptom of severe burn-out that I explain in detail in *Restored*.

The danger is real. Regardless of how intelligent, talented, dynamic, spiritual, or annointed, no pastor is immune, but we *can* and *must* keep them covered!

TAKEAWAY

Pastors are in danger because they are bleeding. They are bleeding from wounds caused by traumatic events. When those wounds aren't properly addressed they can eventually drive a pastor into isolation and detachment. I know that sounds like a steep and rapid fall, and it is, but it begins with bleeding.

I grew up in a blue collar home. My Dad was a master plumber and worked hard to keep his customers happy. Doing his own repairs usually came last. We always joked that a plumber's house always has a leak. Why? Because, Dad put others first. Would you agree that your pastor does the same?

Let me be candid for a moment and say, pastors are used to people "bleeding" all over them, but they will go to great lengths to keep from "bleeding" on others. They know how to bandage your wounds, like a good shepherd would, but they are slow to seek the same for themselves.

Here's what you can do. Firstly, begin to intercede on behalf of your pastor. Secondly, look for areas in which you can do your part to lighten the load your pastor is carrying. Thirdly, let them know, even in small ways, that you care. Fourthly, If you need to "bleed," bleed on someone else for a change. God isn't limited to using only your pastor to minister to you. Fifthly, recruit and arm others with the burden you have and information you've received to lift up the arms of your shepherd.

PRAYER FOR HEALING

Lord, You are our Healer, Deliverer, Strong Tower, and a very present help in the time of trouble. No wound escapes your view, no tear falls to the ground unnoticed. Your Word declares in 2 Chronicles 16:9 that Your eyes run to and fro throughout the Earth, searching to strengthen those whose hearts are fully committed to You. You are a God of compassion and love, with healing in your wings.

I intercede for healing on behalf of my pastor. Father, we recognize that its impossible to fight the good fight of faith without being wounded. You never promised us we wouldn't have afflictions, but You promised You would deliver us out of them all.

May You touch every hurt. May You cause the bleeding to cease. May You turn every painful wound into a healed scar to testify of Your faithfulness.

Gracious God, I pray that you would shield my pastor from hurtful words and actions that are designed to cut and divide. I cancel every assignment of the adversary against my pastor, for no weapon formed against them will prosper and every tongue that rises against them, You shall condemn.

For You, Oh Lord, are our Refuge and Strength. I thank You for showing grace and mercy to bleeding shepherds, as You bind up their wounds and strengthen them for the fight!

7
Because They Get Distracted.

Pastors are in danger because they get distracted. Their attention is in high demand, requiring them to distinguish between direction and distraction. Sometimes the differences are very subtle. Allow me to illustrate using Mary and Martha in Luke chapter 10.

> "As Jesus and his disciples were on their way, he came to a village where a woman named Martha opened her home to him. She had a sister called Mary, who sat at the Lord's feet listening to what he said." (Luke 10:38-39 NIV)

Jesus was in town and accepted an invitation to come to Martha's house for a meal. This wasn't just any ordinary house guest, it was the Teacher, the Rabbi, the Messiah. To host a sojourner was one thing, but to have Jesus as your guest required intense preparation. According to the Jewish customs of hospitality, Martha had certain duties as a hostess to prepare for this illustrious guest.

To the Jews, hospitality was more than just good manners, it was a sacred undertaking to care for the physical needs of the traveller or stranger. The Old Testament is peppered with illustrations of such hospitality. Abraham entertained three strangers in Genesis 18. Rahab entertained Joshua's spies in Jericho in Joshua 2. A man named Manoah and his wife were visited by the angel of the Lord foretelling the birth of Samson in Judges 13. Manoah detained the visitor, unaware it was an angel of the Lord, and prepared a meal, which the angel instructed him to offer as a burnt offering unto the Lord. The Shunammite woman, in 2 Kings 4, prepared a room in her house for the prophet Elisha because she entertained him so frequently. Hospitality was central to their culture.[16]

Martha had work to do. She had to set the table, bake the bread, prepare the dishes, fill the water pots, prepare the food, and set the house in order. Martha is hosting and entertaining the King of Kings and Lord of Lords! No expense can be spared. No corners can be cut. No stone left un-turned. Martha is leaving nothing to chance in preparation for Jesus' visit. She is committed to the task and giving attention to every detail.

I see a pastor in Martha. Like Martha, I wanted to entertain Jesus in the house. I wanted the sanctuary to be filled with His presence when we gathered together. I wanted Him to dwell in the midst of our worship and speak to us through His Word. I wanted everything to be done right and in a spirit of excellence. The table had to be set. The atmosphere had to be created. The building had to be ready. I cut no corners, left nothing to chance, and gave attention to every detail. For pastors and ministry leaders, preparation is important work, but when does the work become a distraction?

> "But Martha was distracted by all the preparations that had to be made. She came to him and asked, "Lord, don't you care that my sister has left me to do the work by myself? Tell her to help me!" "Martha, Martha," the Lord answered, "you are worried and upset about many things, but few things are needed—or indeed only one. Mary has chosen what is better, and it will not be taken away from her." (Luke 10:40-42 NIV)

I want you to read the first four words of the above passage again. *But Martha was distracted.* She wasn't doing anything wrong.

She wasn't being neglectful. She wasn't dishonoring her guest. She was carrying out her duties with fervency and passion according to her culture. Martha was no novice; she had entertained guests before. She knew what needed to be done, how to lay out a meal worthy of a magazine, down to the minutest of details. We often unjustly throw stones at Martha for being in the kitchen instead of at Jesus's feet with Mary. But, Martha was a woman on a mission and Jesus was worthy of a king's reception.

Another misconception we often draw from this passage is that Martha was trading communion with Jesus for works, as if she wished to impress Him rather than worship Him. This is not the case at all. Going back to Jewish custom, after she finished the preparations, she would personally serve him, and give all her attention to him. She was doing things in what she believed was proper order.

Further, when Martha addressed Mary's lack of assistance in preparing, she was equally chastising her for breaking an important rule of hospitality. It was rude for a host to give too much attention to a guest, so as not to make the guest feel uncomfortable. Not only was Mary overly attentive to Jesus, she was sitting at His feet, hanging on every word. It was not how things were to be done.[17]

Martha's hospitality was by the book. You can do things the right way with a right heart and still get distracted. The original Greek in Luke 10:40 is *perispaó*. It is only used this once in all of scripture. It means, "to be drawn away."[18] Now read the verse this way.

"Martha was drawn away by all the preparations that had to be made."

Sometimes the things that have to be done get in the way of the reason for which we do them. The preparations draw us away from the guest. The busyness draws us away from the business. The ministry draws us away from the mission. Distraction is not always dysfunction; sometimes it's a good thing that draws us away from a God thing. Martha was doing a good thing, but Mary was doing a God thing.

Mary was so hungry for what Jesus was saying that she dared to act in a manner that contradicted what was culturally acceptable. She was so captivated by Jesus that she put communion before preparation. Allow me to pose a question. Is it possible that the works of ministry, or what is culturally relevant can sometimes be a distraction? Is it possible that what has to be done can sometimes distract us from living in the moment of divine appointment? I believe the answer is, yes. The Bible says, "Martha was distracted by all the preparations that had to be made." Martha was distracted but Mary was directed.

Notice, Jesus used what upset Martha to get her attention. She was so upset with Mary that she asked Jesus, *"Lord, don't you care that my sister has left me to do the work by myself? Tell her to help me!"* When you are distracted you will sometimes get upset at people who don't share you priorities. In Martha's view, Mary was being inhospitable, but Jesus was about to drop a truth bomb on her.

I believe the central theme of this story is not a question of the validity of Martha's work, but a question of timing. Her preparations had to be made, but Jesus was about to show her that there was one thing that ranked higher than all of the preparations. What she was preparing would feed the body and strengthen it for the journey, but what Jesus was speaking would feed the spirit.

Notice Jesus response. Martha, *"You are worried and upset about many things, but few things are needed—or indeed only one. Mary* has chosen what is better, and it will not be taken away from her." What I hear Jesus saying is, "Martha, you can feed the body, and that's important, but only I can feed the spirit, and that's better!"

Martha was setting the atmosphere but Mary was getting a Word. There is nothing wrong with setting the right atmosphere, but the atmosphere only changes the mind-set. The Word is what changes the heart. Atmosphere without the Word is empty, but the Word doesn't need a certain atmosphere; it stands alone.

Okay, I've taken the long way around to make a point. It is very easy for pastors to get so busy doing the right things with a right heart, making the preparations that must be made, doing the work of ministry, taking care of others, carrying out important tasks, that they become distracted. They are not dysfunctional, just distracted. They are not neglectful, just distracted. They are doing good things, but distracted from God things. Their direction gets clouded by distraction. The result is a pastor who gets so busy that he neglects himself. That's dangerous.

50% OF RESPONDING PASTORS SAY THEY HAVE TROUBLE SAYING "NO".

The reason pastors have trouble saying "no" to folks is because we have a servant's mentality. When I conducted leadership training in my church, I integrated spiritual gifts inventories. I would tell my new leaders that the inventory was not to reveal what their gifts were, but to reinforce and confirm to them what they already know about themselves. Without fail, those who tested high in the servanthood department always had trouble saying "no".

When you say "no", you risk upsetting people. Martha was upset because Mary made a choice between what was good and what was

God. She said "no" to what was important to Martha. Pastors don't like to upset people. When people get upset it can cause unwanted drama. When a pastor has to say "no", they risk the perception that what is important to someone isn't important to them. Obviously that's not true, but people tend to take things very personally.

Did you notice that Jesus did not chastise Martha for working? He just redirected her focus. He said her name twice, "Martha, Martha." Perhaps that's what it took to break her focus. When my son was younger, I often had to say his name two or three times to break his attention from whatever he was doing. Your focus cannot be redirected until it is first broken. I can hear Jesus saying, "Martha, calm down. Don't be upset, just focus on Me."

TAKEAWAY

Pastors are in danger because they get distracted. They become busy doing the right thing with a right heart, trying to meet the expectations that have been placed upon them by the church culture. Like Martha, and in good faith, they are often drawn away by the busyness of the business. They aren't in error. They aren't dysfunctional. They aren't less spiritual. They are just distracted.

Pastors need the space to say "no". They are not doing someone a disservice by saying no. They aren't being untrue to their calling by saying no. They aren't neglecting the ministry by saying no. The ability to say no, even when it might upset someone, puts pastors in position to get a Word, just like Mary. If you want your pastor to give you a Word, they must give priority to getting a Word. That means saying no to distractions.

The adversary will use people as distractions. Unfortunately, sometimes people take advantage of the pastor's kindness and demand their time disproportionately. Pastors need boundaries to prevent those kinds of distractions, otherwise they risk neglecting themselves and their families trying to keep everyone happy. You and I both know how dangerous that can be.

I challenge you to pray this prayer of focus with me.

TEN REASONS WHY PASTORS ARE IN DANGER

PRAYER FOR FOCUS

Father in Heaven, I intercede for my pastor, today. I recognize that in doing the work of ministry, distractions may come. I acknowledge that the demands upon my pastor's time and attention are great, and how torn they must feel when deciding where their efforts are most needed. I ask you to grant divine focus .

Lord, I ask you to expose distractions and areas of ministry that are depriving my pastor of proper focus. Expose the things and people that have been sent by the adversary to steal focus and delay or prevent a breakthrough.

I ask you to break my pastor's focus from anything that may be distracting them from the Word and the direction You are going, and grant them laser focus upon Your face, Your will, and Your plan.

Thank you, Lord, for revealing to me the danger that my pastor is exposed to in the area of focus, and giving me the weapon of intercession to come against the enemy on their behalf.

83

8
Because They Lack Confidence.

Pastors are in danger because they lack confidence. Confidence is fluid. It increases with successful experience and it decreases with every failure. Managing confidence is something I struggled with as a pastor. It's difficult to explain why. Regardless of the affirmation I received from my superiors, peers, and parishioners, I still wrestled with this underlying notion that my ability as a pastor and leader was subpar. As I mentioned earlier, I am hard on myself, constantly feeling my work product isn't good enough. I'm not alone.

67% OF RESPONDING PASTORS SAY THEY ARE CONSTANTLY CRITICAL OF THEMSELVES.

Pastors are facing a cultural challenge that has a big impact on the confidence issue. In previous generations the ministry was given respect. That's not always true today. Pastors often find that the people they are ministering to are the same people who oppose them. One pastor wrote to me these words:

> "It's been said that gossip is saying something behind someone's back that you wouldn't say to their face, and flattery is saying something to someone's face that you wouldn't say behind their back. Pastors deal with both on a regular basis, and often don't know who is really with them or against them."

Another pastor wrote this:

> *"The hardest part of my experience was tuning out the chatter. Being a person with feelings, it's hard to tune it out or ignore it. Pastors do hear the chatter: "You're not a good friend", "I'm not coming back because of what you said", "The chairs aren't arranged how I want them", "You talk too fast", "Why did we do communion after the 2nd song this week? And many other petty things that you later realize don't even matter. People get mad at you for things they wouldn't normally get mad at others for. It's almost a no win situation at times. You simply can't make everyone happy. When you enjoy making people happy, it's a devastating blow to be the target of unhappiness and anger."*

Pastors are fighting an uphill battle, dealing with an entitled, brainwashed, self-centered, society who has neglected their roots. Today's culture gives us churchgoers who want just enough Jesus to make them feel good but not so much that it requires commitment. This has a very large impact on the confidence of a pastor as a human being.

Another factor that affects a pastor's confidence is comparison. The church has become a business model and pastors find themselves in competition with a church culture that is constantly changing. I've gone to dozens of leadership conferences through the years, and left most of them feeling so inadequate that I thought I should change careers and leave ministry to the professionals. With every conference speaker, usually the pastor of an up and coming megachurch, we are introduced to new and innovative ways to do things, that dwarf our efforts in their shadow. Please understand, I'm not throwing stones at mega-church pastors or denouncing new and innovative ministry idea. I'm just saying, regardless of how hard we work there is always someone doing it bigger and better. Pastors have a lot to compete with.

8
Because They Lack Confidence.

PRAYER FOR FOCUS

Father in Heaven, I intercede for my pastor, today. I recognize that in doing the work of ministry, distractions may come. I acknowledge that the demands upon my pastor's time and attention are great, and how torn they must feel when deciding where their efforts are most needed. I ask you to grant divine focus.

Lord, I ask you to expose distractions and areas of ministry that are depriving my pastor of proper focus. Expose the things and people that have been sent by the adversary to steal focus and delay or prevent a breakthrough.

I ask you to break my pastor's focus from anything that may be distracting them from the Word and the direction You are going, and grant them laser focus upon Your face, Your will, and Your plan.

Thank you, Lord, for revealing to me the danger that my pastor is exposed to in the area of focus, and giving me the weapon of intercession to come against the enemy on their behalf.

Now, before you go getting super spiritual on me, I know that ministry is not a competition and that all success comes from the Lord. I'm simply trying to convey the idea that pastors always feel the pressure to be on the cutting edge to remain successful. For this reason we are always examining and re-examining our work, grappling with the underlying sense that it's not good enough.

I will be the first to admit that I'm probably less confident than most, but I don't believe I'm alone. I hear the struggle for confidence in the voices of colleagues when we speak. I even hear it in the words of ordinary men in scripture, chosen to do extraordinary things. Abraham lacked confidence in his ability to father a nation. Moses lacked confidence in his ability to deliver Israel from bondage. Jeremiah lacked confidence in his ability to be a prophet. No one is above the confidence question.

Let me ask you, have you ever lacked confidence? Have you ever compared yourself to someone else and became discouraged? Of course you have; everyone has at some point in their lives. Your pastor is no different. When I compare what I'm doing to the megachurch pastor speaking at the conference, I feel grossly unqualified and ineffective. The problem with comparison is that it is skewed because we are on different laps of our race.

> *"And let us run with perseverance the race marked out for us, fixing our eyes on Jesus, the pioneer and perfecter of faith. For the joy set before him he endured the cross, scorning its shame, and sat down at the right hand of the throne of God. Consider him who endured such opposition from sinners, so that you will not grow weary and lose heart." (Hebrews 12: 1b-3 NIV)*

I love this illustration of the great race. When you begin a race, you know where the finish line is. You don't leave the starting line and randomly wander until you find the finish line. It is a predetermined course. It is "marked out " for you.

When I went to police academy, I had to run a mile and a half in 12 minutes and 25 seconds to graduate. During the first week, we had to do a physical fitness assessment. They took us to a football field equipped with a running track. A mile and a half was about 6 and a quarter laps around that track. I ran two laps and collapsed. Obviously, I was grossly out of shape. Others were running the track like a deer and passing their time requirement with no problem. So what was the difference between my performance and theirs? They had put in the work. They had been stretching, running, and building their endurance. For me to compare myself to the guy running the fastest time was unfair. I couldn't expect myself to perform at the same physical ability because I hadn't conditioned my body yet.

For four months, I ran three to four times per week until I could run the entire mile and a half. Then, I focussed on pace and speed until I could run it under my time limit. The day of the final physical test, I ran with confidence because I knew I could do it. I remember running that track, keeping track of my laps, and knowing I had about two minutes and four seconds to run each lap. I was running in circles, literally, but I knew I had a goal and a finish line. Laps one and two were easy (remember I collapsed after two the first time). On laps three and four I began to get tired. My confidence began to waiver. I began to slow down. I watched as other runners gave up and laid down in the grass. But because I knew I had done it before, I fought through the pain. When I got to lap six, I could see the finish line in sight. My confidence came back and I used every ounce of strength left in my body to sprint to the finish line! In case you were wondering, I passed with 27 seconds to spare.

The moral of the story is, I can't compare myself to the megachurch pastor at the conference because he's on a different lap of his race. What I don't see, when he's on that stage looking successful and blessed, are the pain and failure he's experienced during his race. He is where he is because he didn't quit when he got tired and out of breath. Even when others were dropping out of the race around him, he kept on running. Even when he felt like he was running in circles but not going anywhere, he kept on running. When he fell down, he got back up and kept on running!

The adversary wants pastors to compare themselves to others because he knows it will affect their confidence. If they lose their confidence, he will try to convince them to quit. That's why the writer of Hebrews tells us what to do with our eyes when we're running; fix them on Jesus, not other runners. The Apostle Paul weighed in on the comparison factor.

> *"Each one should test their own actions. Then they can take pride in themselves alone, without comparing themselves to someone else" (Galatians 6:4)*

Comparing myself to others robs me of the joy of small victories. The only person I should compare myself to is the man in the mirror. Say this with me, "I'm not where I want to be, but I'm not where I used to be!" Keeping that truth before you and celebrating your small victories will keep you going when you get weary in the race.

The original Greek in Hebrews 12 which is translated "weary" is *kamnó*. It is also translated "ready to collapse."[19] When I compare myself to others, it affects my confidence and drives me to work toward the wrong goal: to be like the person to whom I'm comparing myself. It leaves me over-worked and ready to collapse. I have to remind myself that I'm not responsible to run like that mega-church pastor, I'm just responsible to finish my race.

A pastor's confidence can also be affected by the affirmation, or lack thereof, that comes from those in their circle. When I'm surrounded by people that believe in me, it lifts my confidence.

42% OF RESPONDING PASTORS SAY THEY DON'T FEEL SUPPORTED BY THEIR SUPERIORS.

The relationship between pastors and ecclesiastical leadership varies. Most organizations have a revolving leadership pool. Superintendents, bishops, overseers, whatever you call them, are usually in place for a limited term. In my experience, it seems just when you get to know them a little and get used to them, their term is up and they are moved on to the next assignment. New leaders bring their own personalities, priorities, communication styles, etc. Because of the revolving system, it can be difficult to form relationships with those over you in the Lord. I'm not criticizing the system, I'm just saying that's how it is, at least in my organization.

In the revolving system, sometimes I felt supported by my superiors and sometimes I did not. Leaders want affirmation from their leaders. Whether they have it, or not, affects their confidence. I want to be clear; when a pastor feels a lack of support from their superiors, it doesn't always indicate a conscious withholding of support. It may just indicate a passive connection in which there isn't much communication between the two. As a former ecclesiastical leader, I may have inadvertently conveyed a lack of support, simply because I did not communicate as much with certain church leaders. The same principle may apply to the pastor-parishioner relationship. I may have left someone I pastored feeling unsupported because of a lack of communication. So the confidence question goes both ways.

Whatever the situation, for a pastor to be successful and lead with confidence, I believe it's important to sense they are supported by their superiors. It's the feeling that if I get in a tight spot, I know someone has my back.

Allow me illustrate using one of my favorite television series, The Andy Griffith Show. There's an episode in which Barney Fife is dealing with two farmers who are illegally selling on the side of the road. The first time he confronts them, they laugh him off and refuse to move. Barney is struggling with his confidence, but he remembered somebody had his back.

He confronts the farmers again, this time with confidence. He again orders them to move their vegetable stand on down the road. They refuse and begin to crowd in on Barney to intimidate him. This time, Barney stands his ground and says, *"You're both a lot bigger than I am, but this badge represents a lot of people. They're a lot bigger than either one of you."*[20] In response, the two farmers turn around and go on their way.

From my perspective, the life lesson in this episode is, when you know someone has your back, it gives you confidence to do a difficult job.

TAKEAWAY

Pastors are in danger because they lack confidence. To summarize confidence in the context of Hebrews 12, let's break it down into three "P's": Performance, perspective, and people.

We all have performed successfully in life at some point or another, whether it's success in business or employment, success in relationships, success in a sport, or whatever. We are all running the race, and we have all experienced a measure of success.

Most pastors don't struggle with performance, they struggle with perspective. How they gauge their performance is entirely based upon their perspective. If pastors are stuck in a rut of unfair comparison, they will never see themselves as successful. As a result, they will struggle with confidence. We have to use the Word of God as the measuring stick to which we compare ourselves.

Our confidence requires people, our support system. Every pastor needs people in their corner, encouraging them and giving them moral and emotional support. Performance, perspective, and people are the keys to a pastor's confidence. Notice, YOU are one of those keys.

PRAYER FOR CONFIDENCE

Oh Lord, I ask you to give my pastor confidence. I pray the promises of Proverbs 3:26 over my pastor, "For the LORD will be your confidence, and will keep your foot from being caught," and Proverbs 14:26, "In the fear of the LORD there is strong confidence, and His children will have a place of refuge." (NKJV)

When my pastor struggles with confidence, I pray that You would be their source of confidence. When they get discouraged and second guess themselves because of unfair comparisons, be an ever present reminder of their daily successes and victories through Your strength. As they contend with the culture of Godlessness, please grant wisdom, resolve, and the confidence to conquer the resistance for the cause of the Kingdom.

Lord, tear down walls of overwhelming expectations that are at the root of the struggle for confidence. Give my pastor endurance to run the race, and not give up. Help me to be a source of blessing and encouragement. Surround my pastor with people who will build up and not tear down.

Finally, I pray that you will give my pastor divine perspective to see their ministry through the lens of Your anointing and power. I pray this in Jesus' name!

9
Because Sometimes They Get Afraid.

Pastors are in danger because sometimes they get afraid. It's unfortunate that people equate fear with faithlessness. Fear is a human emotion that no one is immune to. When Jesus prayed in the garden, "Father, let this cup pass from me," He must have been experiencing fear because of the suffering He knew was to come. Fear is normal. But fear does not have to control one's life. Fear is to be conquered by faith and courage.

When Paul speaks of the danger of his persecution in 2 Corinthians 11, he does not imply that his journey was without fear. He was open about his fear to the Corinthians.

> "And so it was with me, brothers and sisters. When I came to you, I did not come with eloquence or human wisdom as I proclaimed to you the testimony about God. For I resolved to know nothing while I was with you except Jesus Christ and him crucified. I came to you in weakness with great fear and trembling." (1 Corinthians 2:1-3 NIV)

The Greek word Paul uses for *fear* is *phobos*, which literally means, "panic flight."[21] Paul was not trying to sound spiritual as if to say, "I came to you in humble weakness, reverent fear, and holy trembling." No! He was saying, "When I came to you, I was weak and afraid! I was running in fear!"

If this general of the faith and apostle of the Lord Jesus Christ was afraid, I'm willing to bet your pastor also gets afraid. Paul's admission of fear in the above passage is supported by Luke's writing in Acts 18:9-11, when the Lord told him to stop being afraid[22].

"One night the Lord spoke to Paul in a vision: "Do not be afraid; keep on speaking, do not be silent. For I am with you, and no one is going to attack and harm you, because I have many people in this city." So Paul stayed in Corinth for a year and a half, teaching them the word of God." (NIV)

Though Paul was afraid, he didn't allow his fear to influence him. In spite of much opposition, he stayed and kept on preaching for another 18 months! Fear is not the problem; it's just a normal emotional reaction to danger. The problem is allowing fear to dictate your next move.

Experiencing fear is normal, but living in a spirit of fear is not.

"For God has not given us a spirit of fear, but of power and of love and of a sound mind." (2 Timothy 1:7 NKJV)

A spirit of fear is a domination of one's mind set; a hijacking of one's thinking; the voice of the adversary applying fear to every facet of one's life. Someone who struggles with a spirit of fear is imprisoned by the influence of that fear upon their thought processes and decisions. Living in a spirit of fear is exhausting. It's more than just a mind battle; it's a spiritual attack.

I can assure you, even pastors battle the spirit of fear. I have been there, fought the battle, won, and worn the ball cap. If you are fighting this battle, or believe your pastor may be, I encourage you to stand on God's Word.

"Casting down arguments and every high thing that exalts itself against the knowledge of God, bringing every thought into captivity to the obedience of Christ." (2 Corinthians 10:5 NKJV)

I love the way The Message translation words this verse.

"We use our powerful God-tools for smashing warped philosophies, tearing down barriers erected against the truth of God, fitting every loose thought and emotion and impulse into the structure of life shaped by Christ." (2 Corinthians 10:5 MSG)

That's powerful! When you are fighting the spirit of fear, command every lose thought, emotion, and impulse to fit into the structure of a Christ-shaped life!

25% OF RESPONDING PASTORS SAY THEY HAVE A CONSTANT FEELING OF IMPENDING DOOM.

A constant feeling of impending doom is the lingering notion that something bad is about to happen, bad news is coming, the worst case scenario will prevail, etc. On the severe side, It can also manifest as fear of imminent death, the end times, or the end of the world. For me it was the fear that when my phone rang it was always going to be a crisis. I even dreaded going to the mailbox for fear of what was there. I always felt like the other shoe was about to drop, so to speak. This is no joke. It's real, and goes much farther than fear.

This feeling of impending doom is well documented as a possible sign of panic, depression, anxiety, and Obsessive Compulsive Disorder (O.C.D.) It can also precede a serious medical event, such as stroke, seizure or heart attack.[23] You should never ignore this feeling; though it can be a spiritual attack, it may point to something more serious.

I am a living testimony that you *can* overcome the spirit of fear. After struggling for many years, I now live in peace. I sleep well at night, I'm not afraid, and the feeling of impending doom is gone. If you're struggling, there is hope.

"If the Son sets you free, you will be free indeed." (John 8:36 NIV).

In case you were wondering, pastors often deal with fear in many areas. Here are just a few. A fear of failure, fear of offending someone, fear of betrayal, fear of losing a family, fear of falling short of expectations, fear of negative perception, fear of effects of ministry on their family; this list could go on endlessly. The point is, pastors deal with fear like everyone else. It doesn't make them less spiritual or somehow disqualify them from ministry. It just makes them human.

TAKEAWAY

Pastors are in danger because sometimes they get afraid. I'm not talking about a fear of running out of gas or getting a flat tire during a funeral procession (although that is a terrifying thought). I'm talking about the fear that they will miss an opportunity, be misunderstood, fail to meet others' expectations, miss important moments with their children, be unprepared, just to name a few.

These are common fears among pastors and just prove that we are human. Leadership fear culminates in the realization that you are responsible for others and answer to God for how you shepherd the opportunity. When serving as a pastor of people, I want to do well. I want to succeed. I want to help people succeed. I want God to be pleased with me.

God created us. He gave us the emotion of fear, but not the *spirit* of fear. The emotion of fear has a purpose; it is our God-given response to physical and emotional danger that prompts us to protect ourselves. Author, Dr. Tom Morris wrote, "The purpose of fear is to make us act. It's not to make us freeze."[24]

The spirit of fear is authored by the adversary. It is debilitating, distracting, and designed to make you freeze, stopping forward progress. We must take authority over the spirit of fear.

PRAYER FOR COURAGE

Lord, I take authority over the spirit of fear. I recognize that my pastor is human and experiences fear just like I do at times. I ask you to cancel the assignment of the adversary, the devil, to seize my pastor with a spirit of fear for the purpose of stopping forward momentum, growth and victory.

I declare freedom over them to make decisions by faith, to walk out Your will in their lives. I pray that You will reassure them that You are a refuge and strength and a very present help in the time of trouble, and therefore they don't have to fear, according to Psalm 46:1, 2.

In Jesus' name, I rebuke the spirit of fear from my pastor's head, heart, and home. I pray that you will surround them with Your Spirit, and hedge them in with peace and rest. Activate Your power, love and a sound mind, and let fear have no place in my pastor's life.

Lord, I pray that You will remove unrealistic expectations from my pastor's mind, that You will order their steps and place them in the middle of opportunities for ministry on a daily basis. May my pastor continue to be motivated by vision and purpose, and not be snared by the "what if" of the devil! Thank You, Lord, for answering my prayer!

10
Because They Neglect Themselves.

Pastors are in danger because they neglect themselves. This isn't a mere presumption, but personal experience.

We tend to be experts in others' issues, while failing to address our own. Like a plumber with leaky pipes, a cardiologist with a bad heart, a mechanic with car trouble, or a pastor who regularly cares for the needs of others, but neglects their own. Maybe in all those cases, we are so busy working to help others that we don't see our own issue until it becomes impossible to ignore. When a plumber's house floods, he can't ignore the leaks anymore. When a cardiologist has a heart attack, he has to have the heart issue addressed. You get the picture.

Pastor's often neglect themselves until they begin to feel the effects mentally, emotionally, and physically. This is the route to burnout. If your pastor is not taking care of him or herself, they are in danger of encountering a myriad of problems.

33% OF RESPONDING PASTORS SAY THEY DO NOT MAINTAIN A HEALTHY DIET

I'm not qualified to give medical or nutrition advice, but I can share my personal experience with you. The effects of my consistently unhealthy diet went beyond weight gain; they led to heart trouble, gastrointestinal problems, migraine headaches, fatigue, and other symptoms. Unfortunately, in my case, this culminated with a heart attack. As a result, I was forced to address my diet. When I got it under control, some of the issues I was having decreased drastically.

Research suggests 74% of Americans are concerned about their weight, and 65% are worried about getting heart disease due to extra pounds. 18% of Americans believe their diet has nothing to do with their heart health.[25] Pastors must be in that 18%, or at least their habits imply so.

It's important for pastors to maintain a healthy diet. Failing to do so, in my experience, can lead down a slippery slope. I realize ministry is not an overtly physical occupation, but the mental and emotional stress can affect a pastor's physical health as well. Fortunately, many of my colleagues have become more health conscious as of late, and I pray the trend continues.

58% OF RESPONDING PASTORS SAY THEY DO NOT GET REGULAR PHYSICAL EXERCISE.

I would assume that a scientific pole would suggest a higher number. In fact, a Cleveland Clinic publication states 80% of Americans don't get enough exercise.[26] Pastors sit behind desks, sit in their cars, sit in living rooms, sit in meetings, sit at hospitals, sit at conferences, and stand to preach. The only exercise some pastors get is running themselves ragged.

Getting regular exercise doesn't mean you have to get a gym membership at "weights-r-us" or "treadmill world". You can jog, walk the dog, play a sport, among other things. Stereotypically, pastors play a lot of golf; I only consider that exercise if you walk instead of driving a cart. I've done several things over the years (intermittently) to get exercise including, racquetball, running, and weight lifting. Strangely enough, my heart attack occurred when I was in the best shape of my life, but the damage had already been done, and it caught up with me.

Does the scripture address this issue of physical exercise? Of course it does! The Apostle Paul weighs in as follows.

> "For bodily exercise profits a little, but godliness is profitable for all things, having promise of the life that now is and of that which is to come." 1 Timothy 4:8 (NKJV)

> "But I discipline my body and bring it into subjection, lest, when I have preached to others, I myself should become disqualified." 1 Corinthians 9:27 (NKJV)

Paul doesn't put physical exercise at the top of the priority list, but he doesn't discount it either. He acknowledges that it "profits a little." A little, in comparison to godliness, that is. He also said that he disciplined his body. This can fall into the category of physical exercise as well, as it requires great discipline.

My point is, pastors need to be conscious of their physical health like the rest of society. Most are unlikely to do so and it puts them at risk. For most of us, it's not a lack of willingness, but the time factor that holds us back.

25% OF RESPONDING PASTORS SAY THEY DO NOT OBSERVE A REGULAR DAY OFF.

67% OF RESPONDING PASTORS SAY THEY DO NOT TAKE REGULAR VACATIONS.

I've grouped these responses together because they both deal with a pastor's rest. If you worked seven days a week, including holidays and weekends, were on-call 24 hours a day, and never took a vacation, what shape would you be in physically? Mentally? Emotionally? This describes the demand on most pastors and the lifestyle of some. Perhaps this speaks to why some pastors say they constantly feel tired and worn out. No one can sustain that kind of lifestyle, let alone pastors. It will put you in the fast lane toward burnout and/or breakdown.

I recently read the term, "work martyrdom," used to describe the American work culture of success at any cost.[27] Is your pastor a "work martyr"? I was. I struggled with being idle, always feeling as if I was responsible for someone or something, and I had no business taking time off. Hi, my name is Jeff, and I'm a workaholic.

Why is this so dangerous? Because forfeiting your time off will affect your health, physically, mentally, and emotionally. The U.S. Travel Association reports that in 2016, American workers gave up $66.4 billion dollars in benefits alone by forfeiting vacation days. That amounts to 206 million vacation days left unused.[28] But why? Why do people give up their time off? Or, more specifically for my subject, why do pastors give up their time off? The same study states that 43% fear returning to a mountain of work, and 34% say no one else can do their job.[29]

The challenge for pastors is that some in their congregations also feel no one else can do the pastor's job. I sensed that as a pastor, and allowed it contribute to my "work martyrdom.

I'll never forget taking a group from the church on a cruise. We had a great time! At the end of the week, when we arrived at the airport to fly home, I received a call that a precious elderly saint in the church had passed away earlier that week. The family was waiting on me to get home to preach her funeral. I felt horrible that I wasn't there for them. I love to cruise, but from then on I was always afraid someone was going to pass away while I was gone.

In order for this pastoral mind-set of "work martyrdom" to change, there must be a change in the church culture. Unfortunately, there are people who are not in favor of their pastor taking time off. How do I know? Because I've personally pastored such people. It's unfair. It's unrealistic. It's dangerous.

I believe when pastors neglect themselves, it leads to the most staggering response of them all.

83% OF RESPONDING PASTORS SAY THEY ARE BATTLING DEPRESSION.

Pastors are in danger, but may I remind you that they are covered.

"No weapon forged against you will prevail, and you will refute every tongue that accuses you. This is the heritage of the servants of the Lord, and this is their vindication from me," declares the Lord." (Isaiah 54:17 NIV) Conclusion

Conclusion

When you first read the title of this book, you may have thought it to be a pronouncement of doom and gloom. You've discovered that's not the case at all. It is a battle plan, an intelligence report to reveal the enemy's strategies. Armed with this information, you can take up your sword, and go to war on your knees.

The persecution against the American pastor is getting hot. It will only increase as we draw nearer to the coming of the Lord. We have certainly witnessed this in the aftermath of the pandemic of 2020. If your pastor has ever needed your understanding, support, and prayer, it is right now.

The greatest danger to pastors is the temptation to walk away.

83% OF RESPONDING PASTORS SAY THEY HAVE A FRIEND WHO HAS LEFT THE MINISTRY.

I have friends who have left the ministry. I have friends who have expressed to me that they want to leave the ministry. They have recognized the dangers of the pastorate and have asked themselves if it's worth continuing. Is it worth the damage that can be caused to their families? Is it worth the abuse they endure from pious and pharisaical churchgoers? This is the crossroad that many have come to.

However, if there is one thing I know about the kind of people who give themselves wholeheartedly to pastoral ministry, it is that they are not easily dissuaded and they don't go down without a fight!

75% OF RESPONDING PASTORS SAY THEY ARE WILLING TO GO TO COUNSELLING.

As I said from the beginning, not all pastors are struggling and bleeding. I believe, however, that the preceding pages do, with a broad brush, paint an accurate picture of the dangers they face as they walk in their calling. We cannot ignore those who are struggling. We cannot stick our heads in the sand and pretend these issues don't exist, while the adversary works his plot to weaken God's shepherds right under our noses. We cannot stand idly by while bleeding shepherds suffer in silence until it's too late. We must uncover the attack and intercede for the ministry.

Pastors are in danger. But, Proverbs 27:12 says, "The prudent see danger and take refuge." Would you pray this one last prayer for pastors with me?

CONCLUSION

PRAYER FOR REFUGE

Psalm 91 (NIV)

Whoever dwells in the shelter of the Most High will rest in the shadow of the Almighty. I will say of the Lord, "He is my refuge and my fortress, my God, in whom I trust." Surely he will save you from the fowler's snare and from the deadly pestilence. He will cover you with his feathers, and under his wings you will find refuge; his faithfulness will be your shield and rampart. You will not fear the terror of night, nor the arrow that flies by day, nor the pestilence that stalks in the darkness, nor the plague that destroys at midday. A thousand may fall at your side, ten thousand at your right hand, but it will not come near you. You will only observe with your eyes and see the punishment of the wicked. If you say, "The Lord is my refuge," and you make the Most High your dwelling, no harm will overtake you, no disaster will come near your tent. For he will command his angels concerning you to guard you in all your ways; they will lift you up in their hands, so that you will not strike your foot against a stone. You will tread on the lion and the cobra; you will trample the great lion and the serpent. "Because he loves me," says the Lord, "I will rescue him; I will protect him, for he acknowledges my name. He will call on me, and I will answer him; I will be with him in trouble, I will deliver him and honor him. With long life I will satisfy him and show him my salvation."

About the Author

Jeff Wolf is an author and speaker based in Cincinnati, Ohio. He answered the call of ministry and began preaching at the age of 15. He is a graduate of Lee University and an alumnus of the Pentecostal Theological Seminary in Cleveland, Tennessee. He has served almost three decades in ministry and leadership as a national evangelist, lead pastor, and denominational leader. Jeff also served 20 years in the field of law enforcement, beginning as a police chaplain and eventually retiring as a patrol sergeant. He continues to serve his local police department as a volunteer chaplain.

Jeff is well known for his dynamic preaching style in local churches, camp meetings and conferences. He is also an author and the founder and president of Resurgence, Inc., a non-profit organization committed to facilitating healing and restoration in the ministry community.

www.jeffwolf.org

TEN REASONS WHY PASTORS ARE IN DANGER

ENDNOTES

1   Strong's Exhaustive Concordance: New American Standard Bible. Updated ed. La Habra: Lockman Foundation, 1995. http://www.biblestudytools.com/concordances/strongs-exhaustive-concordance/.

2   Strong's Exhaustive Concordance: New American Standard Bible. Updated ed. La Habra: Lockman Foundation, 1995. http://www.biblestudytools.com/concordances/strongs-exhaustive-concordance/.

3   Suciu, Peter. "Does Negativity Drive Users Off Social Media?" Forbes. Forbes Magazine, November 13, 2019. https://www.forbes.com/sites/petersuciu/2019/11/15/does-negativity-drive-users-off-social-media/#6277b4236dfb.

4   Mcdermott, John. "Those People We Tried to Cancel? They're All Hanging Out Together." The New York Times. The New York Times, November 2, 2019. https://www.nytimes.com/2019/11/02/style/what-is-cancel-culture.html.

5   Perkins, Tony. "Like a Tweet, Lose a Lease." FRC. Family Research Council, June 10, 2020. https://www.frc.org/updatearticle/20200610/tweet-lease?fbclid=IwAR1LrPMz_C7Ie1ZAqAntTq3K8fRxWqlLwhlrCgec10b68kUqzCNtcE7dygI.

6   Mayo Clinic Staff. "How Stress Affects Your Body and Behavior." Mayo Clinic. Mayo Foundation for Medical Education and Research, April 4, 2019. https://www.mayoclinic.org/healthy-lifestyle/stress-management/in-depth/stress-symptoms/art-20050987.

7   Tozer, A. W., and Ravi Zacharias. The Radical Cross. Chicago: Moody Publishers, 2015. Pg 26, 27

8   Wolf, Jeff. "The Breakdown." In Restored: Your Minis-

try Can Survive Your Failure, 118–20. Loveland, OH: Resurgence, 2019.

9   Kristalyn Salters-Pedneault, PhD. "Internalized Symptoms With BPD Include Depression and Social Issues," April 13, 2020. https://www.verywellmind.com/internalizing-425251.

10   Kahn, David. Seizing the Enigma: the Race to Break the German U-Boat Codes, 1939-1943. London: Faber and Faber, 2010.

11   U-571. Film. Roma: Universal pictures, 2000.

12   CBS News. "CDC: Nearly 9 Millon Americans Use Prescription Sleep Aids." CBS News. CBS Interactive, August 29, 2013. https://www.cbsnews.com/news/cdc-nearly-9-millon-americans-use-prescription-sleep-aids/.

13   "Sleep Deprivation." Department of Neurology. Accessed July 31, 2020. https://www.columbianeurology.org/neurology/staywell/document.php?id=42069.

14   Wolf, Jeff. "The Golden Hour." In Restored: Your Ministry Can Survive Your Failure, 137. Loveland, OH: Resurgence, 2019.

15   Goldsmith, B. (2018, November 27). How To Best Use Detachment. Retrieved August 12, 2020, from https://www.psychologytoday.com/us/blog/emotional-fitness/201811/how-best-use-detachment

16   Singer, Isidore. "Hospitality/Host." In The Jewish Encyclopedia: a Descriptive Record of the History, Religion, Literature, and Customs of the Jewish People from the Earliest Times to the Present Day, 480. New York: Funk and Wagnalls Company, 1901.

17   Singer, Isidore. "Hospitality/Host." In The Jewish Encyclopedia: a Descriptive Record of the History, Religion, Literature, and Customs of the Jewish People from the Earliest Times to the Present Day, 481. New York: Funk and Wagnalls Company, 1901.

18   Strong's Exhaustive Concordance: New American Standard Bible. Updated ed. La Habra: Lockman Foundation, 1995. http://www.biblestudytools.com/concordances/strongs-exhaustive-concordance/.

19   Strong's Exhaustive Concordance: New American Standard Bible. Updated ed. La Habra: Lockman Foundation, 1995. http://www.biblestudytools.com/concordances/strongs-exhaustive-concordance/

20   Ruben, Aaron. "Lawman Barney." Episode. The Andy Griffith Show. CBS Studios, November 12, 1962. Season 3, Episode 7.

21   Strong's Exhaustive Concordance: New American Standard Bible. Updated ed. La Habra: Lockman Foundation, 1995. http://www.biblestudytools.com/concordances/strongs-exhaustive-concordance/

22   Jackson, Wayne. "Acts 18:9 - Paul's Fear at Corinth." ChristianCourier.com. Access date: August 27, 2020. https://www.christiancourier.com/articles/1079-acts-18-9-pauls-fear-at-corinth

23   Holland, K. (2019, September 24). Can a Feeling of Impending Doom Be a Symptom? Retrieved August 27, 2020, from https://www.healthline.com/health/feeling-of-impending-doom

24   Tom Morris. (2015, August 04). The Purpose of Fear. Retrieved August 27, 2020, from http://www.tomvmorris.com/blog/2015/8/3/the-purpose-of-fear

25   Wheeler, T. (2019, February 04). Americans Concerned About Their Weight, but Don't Understand Link to Heart Conditions and Overall Health. Retrieved August 31, 2020, from https://newsroom.clevelandclinic.org/2019/01/31/americans-concerned-about-their-weight-but-dont-understand-link-to-heart-conditions-and-overall-health/

26   Heart and Vascular Team, Cleveland Clinic. (2019, November 19). 80% of Americans Don't Get Enough Exercise - and Here's How Much You Actually Need. Retrieved August 31, 2020, from https://health.clevelandclinic.org/80-of-americans-dont-get-enough-exercise-and-heres-how-much-you-actually-need/

27   Aalai, A. (2018, April 17). Give Yourself The Day Off! Retrieved August 31, 2020, from https://www.psychologytoday.com/us/blog/the-first-impression/201804/give-yourself-the-day

28   The State of American Vacation 2017. (2019, October 18). Retrieved August 31, 2020, from https://www.ustravel.org/research/state-american-vacation-2017-0

29   The State of American Vacation 2017. (2019, October 18). Retrieved August 31, 2020, from https://www.ustravel.org/research/state-american-vacation-2017-0.

Made in the USA
Middletown, DE
11 August 2024